The Gentle Warrior
Twila Jean Rounds

National Library of Canada Cataloguing in Publication Data

Twila Jean
        The gentle warrior / Twila Jean.
ISBN 1-4120-0604-X
        I. Title.
CS71.E13 2003   929'.2'0973   C2003-903503-4

TRAFFORD

This book was published *on-demand* in cooperation with Trafford Publishing.
On-demand publishing is a unique process and service of making a book available for retail sale to the public taking advantage of on-demand manufacturing and Internet marketing. **On-demand publishing** includes promotions, retail sales, manufacturing, order fulfilment, accounting and collecting royalties on behalf of the author.

Suite 6E, 2333 Government St., Victoria, B.C. V8T 4P4, CANADA
Phone   250-383-6864   Toll-free   1-888-232-4444 (Canada & US)
Fax   250-383-6804   E-mail   sales@trafford.com
Web site   www.trafford.com   TRAFFORD PUBLISHING IS A DIVISION OF TRAFFORD
HOLDINGS LTD.
Trafford Catalogue #03-0973   www.trafford.com/robots/03-0973.html

10   9   8   7   6   5   4

Contents

Poems

Acknowledgments

*Thank you with all the gratitude my
heart can give!.....*
*To all my fellow travelers, near and far,
who were willing to help me grow and
live.*
*To all my relatives and extended families
who need to know how very important
they are. Especially my husband and
children who are a special part of my
soul and volunteered to come into this
lifetime with me. Also my parents for
bringing me into this world!*

(another choice)
**A special blessing to Launa Huffines
and her angelic guides for their
continued and unwavering dedication in
helping us all, by giving us the tools to
understand.*

Books by Launa Huffines
Bridge of Light
Healing Yourself with light
*Tape courses @ Pathoflight.com or call
541-488-1322 or fax 541-482-5891*

Dedication

to those who have gone before her...

Introduction

How do you become a Gentle Warrior when you are so damn angry and hurt? You even feel like you want to kill something! Everywhere you turn there seems to be a wall you cannot penetrate. You are in a cage emotionally and all apparent answers you have sought have been exhausted. You then turn it inward because there seems to be no other way, not realizing that there is.

> *To fly, not to be earthbound*
> *held by the magnet so strong*
> *to break free*
> *this is flight to me*

Why are you so mad? Name a dozen reasons and still the list will not be finished. The same with sad and all other negative emotions we feel. We believe that this is the way the world will stay, as it has for eons and eons. What if someone could show you the way to change all this and really make it work. Sometimes extremely difficult to

11

almost seemingly impossible and unacceptable situations will have you trapped in a mind set of "no way out." It only takes a deep desire within to find our way back to balance. This is where we started and this is where we should be. The following story will explain what you can do about it.

When we seek to lead a more spiritual life we are often our own worst critics. Somehow, we try to be perfect. Well, I am here to tell you that's not going to happen. You will be a much happier person if you say to yourself; "I am, what I am". You might think you don't or cannot love yourself, but you will learn. Now the battle is on! The question is, how can I be a warrior and not hurt others? Where do I begin? You begin at the beginning.

Just follow the yellow brick road...

Choices

Every time you make a decision you have to ask yourself, where is this going to take me? For example, here comes that old fight again and it makes me so mad I could k___! "What's that", you say? Do you want to stop the same old reaction from repeating itself again and again? Does this tell you something! How do we stop this broken record? I have found one solution that works every time. If you don't play the 'Ping Pong" game, it can't happen. That is what happens when someone hits the ball to you, (communication with ulterior motive) and you just don't reply. Now that's really, too easy. See, you just made a choice! My doesn't that feel good! Gee, that's so simple. Can I do it again next time? Can I do it again without anger? Somewhat! Remember we're not perfect. You are only preventing a train wreck! Now that's putting it in terms we can all understand. It's like we have to......

do it over and over again until we get it right. At least that's what I have observed and experienced.

When you really decide not to play the game anymore just put this invisible shield around you and when the ball is hit to you, just let it drop! It takes two to play the game.

Here are a few simple rules to follow:
1. Fight like hell, but fight with the right weapons.
2. Never give your power away to anyone.
3. No one has the right to interfere with another's free will.
4. It isn't love if it's not unconditional. (meaning, I want something in return) Don't we all! Then there are times we are so immersed in darkness and sorrow and we cannot see a way out. No-No-No-No-No! There is a way out! There is a door! There is always a door! Go ahead and scream at your Angels or God or your Spirit guides. You say, 'I don't believe in that!" That's okay, do it

anyway. You say, 'I can't get any time alone" or you're already doing it alone. Do you know you never cease to exist! It's a scie ntific fact that matter never goes away. It only changes form. Suicide won't get you out. If there is anything I have learned, there are some things I don't want to repeat!

That now introduces the reincarnation question. The answer for myself was, I can't possibly get it right in just one lifetime. Remember, it's your choice in all matters. Close your eye's and take a deep breath. (even though your face is wet and your nose is stuffed and you're on the toilet at three am because it's the only solitude you can experience!) Take another deep breath. Now trust the inner you. The intuitive part. That's how you can get help. It's there. It was just all covered up. There now, for just a moment you opened a door.

Breathing is giving,
            is breath
        is life
        is love
        is light
        is all...

Remember, you just gave yourself permission. To control what's going on? No; to release, allow, dump. Rest those weary shoulders and unclench those fists. You gain control when you let go. Why? Because it will bring dis-ease to you if you continue to own this pain! Do you recall the story about matter never going away? Matter is energy. We are energy. Our energy is the world. Don't try to get too technical. There are a million books out there with every possible explanation about life, including this one. I find that somehow I am always led to what book I need to read and what I needed to know at the time. The same goes with people that you meet. 'Nothing by Cha nce," a book by Richard Bach, says it very well.

Abuse is a very sensitive subject. There are all kinds of abuse. Physical, mental and emotional. If this is your situation and children are involved it can get very complicated. There are many subtleties that we do not know are abuse. We put up with situations that we truly don't understand. We keep thinking things will change or get better because we have this innate ability to start over. You see we have things within us that we have not yet faced or dealt with. Oftentimes the other person does not know how to deal with it at all. Somehow that pressure valve has to be released. Usually it is released on others or any other way we can find to release it.

One of the habits we have that keeps putting us back into the same situations is negativity. Nine times out of ten we will discuss what is wrong with the world, rather than what is right with it. It seems to be a blanket of protection around us, so that we do not have to face our own problems. What we are really doing is putting fences around ourselves and others. They in turn are doing the same to us. We build them higher and thicker until we lose sight of the light within. What a picture! If we could stop to think and listen, we could tear down those fences. What happens when we take them down? You start to say positive things, more light comes in and now you have an open mind. No matter what or how you believe, take down those fences. All negativity is a fence. No wonder we feel trapped. We are! Kick down those fences that you or someone else put up.

Your mind is a free gift. It's your birthday present! Spend it the way you want to. Now that you have your mind back, (at least for the moment) let's fill it with something positive. Let's say, I'm in the beautiful process of preparing to receive my gift of_____. You fill in the blanks. This way you can have any positive thing you want. The more you fill it with beauty the more beauty you have in your life. Now all we have to do is practice!

A very dear friend of mine wrote the following words for me and I have kept them tucked away in my personal things. I wish to share this with you.

"Today is mine! It is unique. Nobody in the world has one exactly like it. It holds the sum of all my past experiences and all my future potential. I can fill it with joyous memories or ruin it with fruitless worry. If painful recollections of the past come into mind or frightening thoughts of the future, I can put them away. They cannot spoil today for me. It is mine! You must remember you are somebody. Never stoop below what you really are. Cling to your ideals, your hopes and your basic principals. If you have to depreciate yourself to belong, then the group to which you want to belong is not worth it!"

Ruth, 1932-1987

19

Guilt / Free Will

There is no guilt, only lessons learned. Sometimes we have to repeat something over and over again until we are through with that lesson. Do not let anyone put a guilt trip on you. I cannot excuse malice of forethought, but it is not mine to excuse. Let me explain. If you are training a child or an animal to learn a new experience it will take time and repetition, because they do not understand their lesson yet. Why do we not give that person the same time and patience? How can we be non-judgmental if we do not pass it on? We do not and cannot understand the situation. We have to let it go! Remember, there is a seed of light in every person. I do not pretend to have all the answers. Watch your words and your thoughts. Just when you thought you understood it was, "what we said," that made the difference, I had to throw in 'thoughts" too! When I realize that I am going in the wrong direction with

either; I say to myself, "stop!" Then I
replace the empty space with light and
laughter. Then, for the moment, I have
won a small battle. What a concept!
What a relief to know we do not have to
carry those burdens anymore. No one
passes judgment on you except yourself.
Free will is a gift! It is your birthday
present! Hard to accept, isn't it? Think
about the fact that no one can change
you except you! Easier said than done!
Now how do you really do it? You make
a choice to open another door. Make a
small decision to walk through them one
at a time.

Have you ever forgiven anyone for
anything? Have you ever forgiven
yourself for anything big or small? Is
there a fence somewhere preventing you
from this act of kindness? Well, if only
you can do it for yourself, is it necessary
for you to do it for someone else? Yes!
Why? Because you learn to release
control and allow and then that fence
has fallen. Oh, you can pick it up again
and we often do but the more often you

do this the easier it is to leave that fence down. This is true freedom. It really helps you to breathe more softly. Oh, what a weight off your shoulders! Now, I will help you to remember a most important fact. Pay close attention to this; especially for those of us who have practiced control most of our lives.

If you feel you are not able to do this by yourself, all you have to do is ask your guardian Angel or your higher power to do this for you. For you, at this time in your human form are unable to do it. It will be done! You might pick that fence up again because you think it is your security. One day you will know that you no longer need that fence to protect you. Actually it was just keeping you a prisoner!

What makes us lonely even when things are going well and we can't seem to shake that feeling? It's our disconnection with our God / Goddess power, soul, oneness. We have separated ourselves over time and we feel lost. We are! We can get back! It's all about priorities. Make a list of yours. If it's like mine used to be it had every priority backwards. I didn't even remember to say a prayer of thanks very often. I just had too much to do and not enough time. I thought that I did not have enough time to allow for spiritual mediation / prayer. Then I discovered that my thoughts, were prayers. This is one of the reasons we have separated ourselves. We have forgotten what is really important. Now let's talk a little more about loneliness. When you meditate or pray you open your heart and fill it with divine love and loneliness has to leave. There is no room for it. Even if it's only for a s hort time. Now all we have to do is get a cork and plug it in so it doesn't slip away! We are still in these human bodies and we are still struggling to get ourselves back on track. Picture a pendulum swinging back and forth; center being where we belong. Sometimes we have to be kind to ourselves and realize that we are not perfect. We just want to tip the scales to

51%. Then we begin to tip the scales in favor of "JOY."

Heartbreak

Heartbreak comes from joy and sorrow. They seem to go hand-in-hand. Most people have experienced it. We would all be millionaires if tears were liquid gold. Do you remember someone promising that there would be no more tears? We have gotten so used to it that we are sure it can't possibly be true. Have you ever made the statement "my heart is breaking" or "you bro ke my heart"? Be careful here! You can actually have the effects of what you are feeling and saying. Now, how do you handle that one? We were always taught how to handle things. Picture a big sign, "you don't have to." Well, who is going to if we don't? Th e person who is having the experience is supposed to do that job. This does not rule out our support and caring as long as you don't take on that responsibility. In terms of terrible things that happen; all of us will have trouble with this. We can change things by....

restructuring the way we act/re-act. Beautiful things happen when we first discover what we have been practicing really works. Wow! The first time I was able to live in the present and not in the past I really couldn't believe it. Even if it was only a short while-- I did it! The one saying that really helped me the most was that, anger comes from the past and worry comes from the future. Well at least I found out where those two belong. The other was something I read. It was, "you deserve to be happy." I wanted to be happy. I could make other people happy. Why wasn't I happy? The question is, do I love myself? Yes, with a little reserve. Now ask yourself again. Do I really love myself? Now were getting down to it. You've got to help yourself first. It doesn't mean you have to stop living while you get yourself perfect. That is not the goal. The goal is searching, learning and growing.

Heartbreak really does come from trying to control life. I find that if I allow and let go, I do much better. How can I learn to do this? Picture a soft rose colored cloud of protection around you. Picture this as divine love. The Angels will help you. All you have to do is ask. Take a deep breath, close your eyes, let go and ask. When we allow them to serve us, they can perform wonderful things for us and often they will clear a path. They will never interfere with your free will. This means we have to trust. Easy to say, sometimes hard to do. It takes awareness and practice and practice and more practice!

I fell in love and then I fell in love with the pain. Now that's a stopper! Can we all identify with that statement? Wait a minute. Does this mean we actually love pain? I don't want to be in pain. Is it a necessary part of our life? We have been taught that it is. There are two choices we have that I recognize at present. One is to build a wall around the pain and never let anyone in. Now that sounds really safe. We are only protecting ourselves. Well I have to tell you that there is a very big glitch in doing this. In trying to protect ourselves we create a physical condition that is harmful to our bodies. This is not unconditional love. It is control and reaction. If we keep doing this, little by little we close off our connection to our oneness of life. This is what some call our light center, Christ center or whatever you need to call that spirit of creation, that I believe, is in all of us. Is this what happens to someone who takes their own life? How much pain did that person cover up and tuck inside? When you do this you own the pain and the results. We are energy and negative energy is harmful! I can understand that!

The second way I see to handle it is again, put up that cloud of positive energy and that keeps the negative energy out of our electrical field. Picture that negative energy bumping into that rose -pink stuff and falling to the ground. Not sending it back because we truly don't want to harm anyone. It sounds so easy. It only takes persistence to get rid of those ancient habits. We

might ask ourselves how long have we
been doing this? It's been way too long!
How do we solve something that is so
very complicated? At least it seems that
way. It only takes unconditional love.
We do have the potential for it. If you
practice and really practice it faithfully
for thirty days you can drop one
negative habit at a time. Now, can I do
anything for thirty days straight!

Life

While under a tree, I question the
journey of life
where, when, why..

like the rising sun, joy
or pain felt to the deepest part of thy
being

the glimmer of a flame deep within
that holds the knowledge we try to reach

bright sometimes, then to go dim

of thyself where is the answer..

shall I but die...

Healing Wounds

Do you know how much it hurts when you get a cut on the tip of your finger? It takes a long time to heal because it has to heal from the inside out. Well that's how it is when we have been wounded in any way. We've been practicing covering wounds for a long time. They just stay there, stuck in our bodies and our energy fields. The Band-Aids we have been applying apparently work but the wound lies dormant, so to speak, until it is triggered again; always trying to get out because it never healed in the first place. Write down the things that keep repeating themselves in your life and you have an unhealed wound from this life or another. How do we do this? First recognize it. Read books on self help, meditate and seek spiritual and professional help, if you so decide. Always know you can heal yourself by having the willingness to do so. You only have to do this for today and then you let tomorrow take care of itself. It is your perspective of how high the mountain is for you to climb. You only have to do today! The one you are residing in right now! Sometimes this comes only after a lot of mental and / or physical pain. It is very real.

Here are some of the Band-Aids that we use to cover up our wounds. Criticism of others and ourselves are two of the big ones. Of course it's 'their" fault. They did this to me. Why? To help you heal all your wounds. Remember when we said it isn't love unless it's unconditional? Well if it is unconditional, it doesn't have any conditions! When the arrows are shot at you and you are surrounded with that beautiful cloud of divine love, you are protected. It takes what? Lots of practice! (there goes that word again) It does work. Walk down the street and give a smile. That's it! Here we go again! It sounds so easy but can become complicated when you are living with someone else. That's the real test and you both set it up! Now, wait a minute!

Why would I do that? The answer is simple. It's so we can quit running around in circles, chasing our tails and begin to grow into a more spiritual and much happier race. See, we do have the answers and the power. We may not like them. We may not accept them. If it is a truth it will work! Yes, we can still have fun, only it will be more pleasant and less painful. We are supposed to have fun! The world was created to be a happy place! We have conditioned our thoughts and our words to say that the world will never change. We have had wars forever and we say, 'it has always been this way and always will be." This has got to stop. We all have to change our ways of thinking and speaking and we can start with ourselves. We leave everyone else to their own responsibility of self growth. Gee whiz! I thought it was my job! Did you? We change ourselves first and little by little, the world will change. You are the world! The world of humanity. You just watch it happen! Now, you become a 'Gentle Warrior." Soon all the junk begins to fall away. I have to remind myself of this all the time. I only have to make this day joyful and beautiful. Not yesterday, not tomorrow. Now, is the only moment I can live in. There were many days I could not find this pleasure. Meditate and speak to our helpers. The wounds will start to heal and life will begin to be as it should be, in balance.

Smile

If I can make you smile today
with jewels that I have brought

While others pass the time away
caring with no thought

A gift I have for you
no greater one can there be

Than to look upon your face and see
what you have really given me...

Gentleness

You must be as gentle with yourself as you would be with a baby kitten. You must care and nurture your heart with the earth. Sit on the ground and feel the earth. Plant sunflowers and take time to start living at a slower pace. You don't have to make everything right for all the people in your family or the friends you have or anyone else! Be a child sometimes. Break the mold that you think society has you locked into. Live each moment as you do when children are sleeping. I remember that short, peaceful time. Relax, even if you don't have children around. Close your eye's and connect with Spirit. Ask for blessings. The gentleness will follow. This is a gift to you and others. It is like a cool drink of water for those who thirst. It is worth far more than gold you can amass. Listen to the still small voice inside and it will tell you what you need to know. Just be quiet and listen. It sometimes comes for only an instant and

at other times it is very strong. Open
your day with Spirit and make your
connection by taking in a deep breath,
closing your eyes and allowing. That, is
your permission. Then send all that
positive energy out to the world. It goes
out like little ripples in a pool. It is a gift
to you and others. You must have a
space where you can be alone
sometimes. It can be in your car, the
bathroom, a trailer or just sitting under a
tree. Touch the grass or water if you can.
Keep any kind of pet, even if it is a
goldfish. If not, feed the wild birds and
they will come. If you are a working
person, picture an invisible jacket
hanging outside your home. Take it to
work with you and when you come back
home, hang it outside and leave your
concerns there for the night. Call it your
invisible worry tree or make a real one.
However, the invisible one is strong
enough to hold it for you until morning.
Try not to take it in your home. Maintain
the sanctity of your home. It doesn't
matter if it's a car, trailer or palace. This

time is yours. If you have children you may have to do this after they are in bed. Rest your soul. Play soft music, run a bath, meditate, read a poem or just be. Think of someone who helped you today by doing something nice for you. Perhaps they said something that helped you and made your day a little easier. Maybe it was something that will stay in your mind and you will always remember. Now, think of a special person in your life who will bring a smile to your face. This can be either in the past or the present. Remember, this is a fellow traveler along the way. Think on that and you will find a peaceful moment. If you have not had any of these things just create one for the future. Color a picture in a coloring book or draw one. Cuddle a teddy bear, sing a silly song or write a page on anything. Watch the birds trying to mate in the spring. That's really special where I live, because the doves have me exhausted just watching them try. One day I actually saw them complete the act and I almost applauded. The male 'bounce's" around endlessly pursuing his mate to be. It's a wonder we have any doves at all! Do these things that I have mentioned, when you are sad and lonely. Write special sayings on a piece of paper and put them in a bowl. Draw one each day. Then read them and you will build a bridge of gentle moments. You will feel the difference and so will all the people around you.

From the heart, flowers

From the hands, messages

From the body, a gift of giving

From the feet, a will to bidding

From the mouth, the golden words

From the ears, a precious hearing

of these, which is the greatest..

The eyes,

for they tell the truth...

Rejection / Acceptance

Any time you sacrifice one person for the good of all, in any given situation, I feel we have lost. If you have to remove yourself from this kind of a situation, at least in your conscious mind, you have made your choice to do what you have to for your own survival. You do this when you know you need to stay in your physical body to help and aid humanity. For without growth from lessons, we are just standing in water up to our ankle's, knee's, waist, neck or over our heads. Let's say that water represents emotions. Positive when you are swimming freely without fear and negative when you are frozen, not moving or drowning.

This reminds me of a sign I read in my doctor's office. It read "death is very still, keep moving." Do you know where you are? Do you like it? Most likely not, if you're reading this book. Watch your words and thoughts. Spend them as precious jewels as water for those who thirst. This is what Jesus taught. Everyone wants to belong. No one wants to be left out. This is our human nature and thought form. We are all going back to the basis of our foundation, which is our unconditional love and our oneness.

It is painful getting there and it is lonely at times. Some of us get to the point where we say, 'this is too much!" Whatever way you choose to grow, is up to you. You do have the gift of free will. Listen closely to that still, small, voice inside you. Give yourself some time to come down from crisis. Then when you are thinking more clearly you can hear it. Again, ask! We do not stand alone. The helpers are waiting for your permission to help. It seems so simple. We are the ones who complicate things. Yes, it can be emotionally painful because we are not yet swimming in the waters freely. Is that hard to understand? We need to learn to merge our soul with our personality so we are, that 'still small voice." That is the voice that makes lovely, wonderful ripples in these waters of life. Drop a pebble of joy in and see how far it goes. It goes forever! We can change the world around us. You are changing things by becoming that which you wish the world to be. We are only taking tiny steps and sometimes a great leap, to share our wonderful gifts.

Promises

May the spirit of joy be with you today
for all of your troubles will soon fade
away

the sadness, the crying, the tears that
you've shed
will soon be the flowers, for the crown
on you head

the fragrance and colors, much greater
than gold
will be the pearls that you wear, in the
heart of your soul

the master he whispers, come safely to
me
with arms to lead you and blessings to
see

I will not fail you and never shall move
with Angels to guide you, in all that you
do

the peace you are seeking, I hold in my
hands
come drink from the waters and never
thirst again...

Anger / Depression

Just when you think you have it all under control, (there's that word again) it jumps right back in your face. You thought everything was fine right where it was. Just when you were getting a handle on coping with life and even giving a little smile once in a while. "By George, I think I've got it!" Everything was just starting to fall into place. Then "POW," your electrical energy field shoots out sparks of anger! You don't care anymore and you find yourself saying, "just make my day." Someone is going to get it and I don't care who! Look out! Here comes that buried anger/depression again. Depression is anger turned inward. If you are depressed, you are angry because you think you can't control what's going on. It has to come out or you will get sick and/or you eventually die! Why am I allowing this to happen to me? It is because we are following our nature as we have always known it to be? It's familiar, it's a friend, it's security, it's

44

you! Well now, maybe you do like you! We own that part of us. It feels good and secure and at least it anchors you! Strong will and seemingly weak will at times but nonetheless, it is yours and you will hang on till death! OOPS! Is that why we die? Is it because we are unable to change? Do we really want to change? The first answer I get from myself is no! (now that's my stubborn self answering without hesitation) On second thought, when we are in deep pain and have had enough, the answer becomes yes! We have to come to that point to be willing to think about it. Here comes that human nature again. When we start getting all our "ducks" lined up and feel better we say "maybe we don't need to change all that much."

That reminds me of an old movie. "The End," with Burt Reynolds and Dom DeLuise. When Burt finds out he is not really dying, he goes through all sorts of comedic/tragic scenarios. In the end he swims out to the ocean to drown himself. Burt goes under for a very long time until you are sure he is gone. Then after what seems to be an excruciating passage of time, he bursts out of the water and screams to the heavens 'I don't want to die!" Then he frantically starts swimming back to the shore, talking to God and bargaining all the way. He promises that he will give 100% if he lives. Then about halfway back he has a change of heart and says he will give 50%. When he gets close to the shore he changes his mind and offers 10%! Then he says 'I want to point out that nobody gives 10%." Can we identify with that? You see, inwardly and outwardly we beg for help when we are in crisis. When the crisis dims we soon forget what brought us to that point. Talk about human nature! The real question is; wherein lies the answer? Anywhere you seek it. Here is one of the methods that works for me. Just close your eye's, take a deep breath, connect with spirit and just be still for awhile. Then I say, "Be still and know that I am God." Make some sort of sanctuary where you can be quiet and alone. Then give yourself permission to rest for a while. It isn't always easy but if something inside you says things should be better and you know it, just keep seeking and guidance will come. Everyone has their truth inside them. The real truth will lead us all to the same beautiful place, be it inward or outward. It will bring peace, if only at times and we can only follow where our inner guidance will lead us. Follow your first impression, no matter how slight. What happens when, because of our circumstances, we are unable to do that? The answer I have found for myself is, that the timing is not right. There is a time frame for us either to play catch-up or for other elements to fall in place. That's why it is so im portant for us to ask for a path to be cleared. Picture this project being built and prepared for our use when the time is right. It would be great if we could just wave a magic wand and all would be done. All things take time and preparation on this side or the other. When we seem to be standing still and nothing seems to be happening; we get exasperated and run out of patience. No answers, no clues, just nothing. We can't seem to get it together. Things have to fall into place one by one. We must learn to have infinite patience.

Anger / Frustration

Anger is good. For heavens sake don't bury it. Work it out, talk it out and fight it out, but with the right weapons. It will relieve you for awhile. Here we go again repeating the same action/ re-action and spilling our energy all over the place. Have you ever seen the movie 'Ground Hog Day"? The movie starred Bill Murray. It's a classic. It says more in that movie than I can ever express on these pages. The first time I saw it I was a little bored with it all and thought it was silly. Then I watched it a second time and then a third time with an open mind. Finally I realized that he kept repeating the same day over and over again until he understood what he needed to do to make it stop. What is in your life that you keep repeating and what part of this makes you angry? When we're angry it is usually directed at someone or something else as I have said before; such as the government or the person you are closest to and even ourselves. This is the blame-game, that we all know very well. Then I repeated an action that was giving me trouble. Really, the trouble was how I was re-acting. I proceeded to map out in my mind, fuming all the while, what I would say and how I would say it. I regressed to past experience, future outcome and yet, I would be in control by damn! It took me three or more days to vent mentally all that was boiling inside. I knew from what I had learned that I needed to stop. I even did this between meditations. Where was the solution?

Truth

What is truth..
is it a dichotomy
are truth and untruth the same

is there only one path
or perhaps all paths lead to the same

Hence, why the downward spiral
to set the least flickering of not hope
but the true reality not to be erased

Can this be the breaking through
no longer to wait in hopelessness
realizing that it must come into balance

No! not will I be convinced otherwise
like the soul within the soul
never to be destroyed

Oh, would others try to change your
thoughts
like beguiled vipers, sure of themselves

to scream it all to no avail
and end in nothingness

51

to leave intact the foreverness
of what is sure and always has been

so easily seen now as we rise with open
arms
and truth of heart
to our beginnings as home to us

the true hearth of oneness and poetic
bliss of our human and spiritual being

joined together,

forever...

Here is what I believe to be the
answer. By living in the soul, we are
living in unconditional love. I'm still
working on this one and will continue to
do so. It is a never ending process with
many hills and valley's. What I try to do
for now, is to keep those hills and
valley's from going to the extremes. I
ask again, for help. I have to keep
reminding myself because we seem to

think we have to do it all alone. When we write things down to release them it helps us to focus on what are the most dominate thought's in our minds, most of the time. Ask yourself if it is positive energy you are using or negative. It will help you to keep things in perspective. What you reach for from your 'inner light" is where you are and where you want to be. We have very clever ways of hiding this light. We cover it up with our personality; you know, the part of us we use when others are around. This is the part of us that makes us think more highly of ourselves. To make sure we are well respected and liked and favored over others. I certainly have. Picture this; you standing on a line with others above you and others below. Reach up and bring them closer and then reach down and bring them up. Ta- Da! That is equality! What a visual! Now that's a challenge!

Grateful Blessings

Have you ever seen on television or in peoples lives, where so much has happened to them that you don't kn ow how they have survived or even cope with their situation. How can they see anything bright? Well if you have been there, and we all have in some way or another, the crisis you are living is very real and it doesn't seem to make any difference how you rate it. It's big to you because you literally can't see the forest for the trees. When you are able and have reached a point where you realize you are re- acting, (repeating) the scene in your mind or on stage, (real life) remember to stop and re-write the scene. Again allow yourself to be the director of your life as it is right now. Forget, at least for the moment, the past and the future and only deal with right now! Anytime you are sad or depressed you are not in the present. You are thinking about what you are going to do about something or why things could not have been different. Then, you plan on how you're going to handle it. No! Breathe, re-write, allow. One of our most frequent pastimes is playing God. Don't misunderstand me. This is really tough! I thought that by being a mom, it was my job to direct. Of course, sometimes we have to smile at our folly. It takes time to change our ancient patterns and some of our traits. It can be done and things can change. Look at me! If I can get anything through this thick head of mine, anyone can! This is one of my strengths. You have one or more also. Sit down and make a list all of yours. Do it right now! See your power and where some of it lies! Here is where you can start to direct you, in a positive action! You have the power to do this as one created, not by accident but with a purpose! If you do not agree with me, that's perfectly okay. Then you are also free to search for your truth.

Sometimes I am a loner. It's okay but we need to realize that being a loner and being alone are two different things. As a loner I sometimes pull away to avoid conflict and pain. When I am being alone and I love it, I am in joy. We are all one as humans, being. That is a fact that we can all see. That is step one. In that alone we can see the oneness of us all. You can be in your own power and still be connected to all that is. We all think we can do it by ourselves. We still have our independence when we stay connected to the light source. It's just like a light bulb. You have to turn it on to see clearly! When you let this light shine through you, it takes away the darkness.

When I repeat myself, it's so I will hear it again and hear it more clearly. Then slowly it begins to stay in my thoughts until the good habit replaces the bad one. Some say that there is no good or bad. Well I just haven't come that far yet! This is what works for me, for now! When you recognize yourself, at least realizing that you have changed something for a moment, you are on your way to making a better place for yourself and others. We all want that! Of course this ripples out to others. Notice what others are talking about. If it's negative, see if you can change your thoughts to something positive. That way we can at least try to keep the game balanced! As we bring in more positive energy, we allow more light (help) to come in. Why? Because we asked for changes. This in turn brings more understanding. Sometimes a crisis makes us so miserable that we open our hearts and listen. When we do manage to extricate ourselves from the 'trauma/drama" or our situation we learned a thing or two. We have to be careful not to drift back into complacency. Why do we do this? It's like an old familiar chair. You just sit there and do nothing. There's nothing wrong with being there. It's just another choice we have.

Are you happy? You deserve to be happy. When you live in a positive moment, you are happy and that's what it's all about. Somewhere along the trail we got off the track. Our security is living in our true nature. It is much more pleasant. You can feel it when it's right. We teach our children boundaries so that they will have a good life. They do go out of their boundaries and then their lessons begin. When they "right" themselves, they have grown. Those who flounder and flip and flop all over the place are crying out for someone to set boundaries for them. Without structure, they have no security. Think of loving arms around us. That is what everyone needs to feel. The magic words for grateful blessings are, "please" and "t hank you". That's why we give thanks for our blessings. We need to sit down and make another list for that. How do we stay in that comfortable space ? I have found that helping someone else takes our minds off our own problems and keeps gratitude alive! It's sometimes hard to believe that everything happens for the best. I don't want to hear that. Without pain we would not know joy. I believe the more we stay in joy, no matter what, the happier we are. We spend lots of time in the other space. All we have to do is reverse it. Break the old habits and keep the good ones. I know this can be very illusive. I am very thankful for all the people in my life that have helped me when I was apparently drowning and did not have the strength to help myself. I see now that they also had their own struggles but were using their compassion and knowledge to help others. Sometimes our negative side cannot possibly see what there is to be thankful for. Give thanks even if you don't feel it and watch what happens. We most certainly would not change unless we truly wanted to. We would not attract the situations that force us to seek more knowledge and for others to be in our lives. Why do we bother? Human nature. We instinctively know who we really are and we keep working our way back to the beginning...

Hello God

Is God really there? I know he is
within me a knowledge of the past
yet so hard to touch upon

a journey of many lives, so long ago
the gathering of the good and bad,
joy and sorrow

to touch upon my memory lightly,
yet so firmly
not shouted loudly but held within,
needing to break free

to open the door for others to see,
while they are still blind

an inner peace, yet unrest
to do thy will, yet turmoil within

a slip, a mistake, only to correct
a given life, almost taken away
so sad, but a joy within

Hello God, I know you're there...

Criticism / Praise

Criticism stings like the sting of a scorpion! Keep that in mind when you do this. It hurts everyone! We are not only inflicting pain, but we are also making fun of someone's search for growth. That sure puts it in a different light! It's our feeble at tempt to make ourselves look and feel better, at the expense of another human, being. It over-shadows the light in the other person. But it feels so good to be right and they really deserve it! How long does it takes us to learn this? I need a little plastic hand to slap myself every time I do this. We get together and are so eager to join in on the task at hand; which is usually destroying someone else's energy. We think it's fun to say, "leave them alone and they will do it all by themselves". Here we go again. Conducting, ruling, heaping piles of that dark stuff, on someone who may be very vulnerable, at that time. We may not have a clue as to when someone is ready to throw in the towel or just ready to crumble. We do not know what brought them to this point. The hardest thing for us to do is walk away and allow--just simply allow. That is unless you want to play the game of "Ping Pong," again and again and ----now you're getting the idea.

Here is a riddle that I think we all know. Pete and Re-Pete were sitting on a fence. Pete fell off and who was left? Re-Pete! etc. A little bit of nonsense is what it's meaning is. No - sense. Okay! Now, what is the soul solution? It's so simple. Praise! Oh! my God! Do I have to? No, only if you want to change you and the rest of the world. Some do and some don't give a darn! That's their free will, divine privilege and right. It takes a long time to think of a way to praise someone we really don't like or perhaps we think we hate. There will be things there to praise, if you look hard enough. If you can't see this; imagine again that person with a strip of tape over their mouth. Now with just a little

bit of quiet, look inside-- way deep--
inside. That's where the Christ center is.
The divine spark was put there by the
Creator. The only problem was his light
got all covered up by this thing called
life. Just think of the power that you
have to give light and love, to someone
who may desperately need it. Then they,
with your words of praise, can begin to
peel of the layers of hurt, criticism,
anger, fear and loneliness. It will all
come back to you with the same results
as it had for that person. It's a much
better way to live life. Cover your ears if
you have to, and walk away in peace.
Change the subject if you can. Say
something encouraging. Drop the
'holier -than-thou" attitude. Who me?
Yes, you, me, anyone. We are all most
definitely in the same boat.

Oh! before I forget, you had better pull
the imaginary tape off your fellow
traveler. Give a little smile and calmness
to all. Look beyond the outer layer.
Envelop them with that rose-pink cloud.
See the Christ light and help them to

brighten it. It was that way in the
beginning. It was promised and we can
prove it to ourselves. Watch the changes
and you will believe in miracles.

Fear / Courage

Fear is an illusion. Then why does it sometimes consume our lives? Whatever negative energy you express comes from fear. Were we there? Were we both good and evil? Where did that fear come from? A long time ago or just yesterday? We couldn't have mucke d up things that badly in just one lifetime. It just doesn't make sense. Where did all this knowledge come from that seems to be innate in us? From God, in just one experience, in just one lifetime? How do we explain about someone's learning process, that dies early in life? What about, what goes around comes around? We keep chasing our tails and history repeats itself. If we have done things that are not for the good of all, who does the judging? Please feel free to draw your own conclusions. The ones you find in this book are mine. I'm sure I have more to learn. Go inside yourself for the answers. Do not let, what someone has told you, be the answers.

You decide. Take back your God/Goddess power. When you do that you just might find your own answers. We all give our power away daily by trying to please others and boosting our own egos. If it involves your own ego you had better back up and take another look!

If everything is going smoothly in your life, you may be treading water or making it smooth by not making any waves. If you don't make waves, just take a little rest for awhile. Then, make a few waves and see what happens. This might certainly throw you into fear. Anger is fear. For many lifetimes you have been fighting literally for your life. How do I know? I keep seeking and learning and finding my own truth. How do you find courage? Well you have to trust that the whole truth will win. I can't tell you how many times I have meditated on trust. I knew that intellectually it was a truth. I knew it would work, but how did I really learn to trust? I learned by letting go and not giving up. When I was hanging by a thread and found that it was it a rope, I learned to trust. By filling up with God's love, I learned to trust. If we know how to love, we take a deep breath and then make it unconditional love. This can be elusive. This little exercise will get you back on track. It is easy to remember and to do. Write down your little successes so that you can see your progress. Whom did you not step on today, either verbally or mentally? Who did you praise and possibly shore up. Don't forget, first and foremost, you must do you! You refine yourself as you would a fine tool. The more you use it, the more you learn your trade.

When I first began, I had no idea how to go within. I couldn't even keep my mind from jumping all over the place, let alone clear my mind. What a joke! Then I started to learn about that which I have told you. Take the first step and it will lead you to the next. Sometimes, there will be lot's of tears. Take a break once in a while and go see a funny movie or read any of the books by Barbara Johnson. One of them is, "Mama Get the Hammer There's a Fly on Papa's Head." The title alone will make you laugh and you will have a better understanding of how to get through life. I often get too serious. Keep your sense of humor! It will keep you going no matter what!

I sometimes get very excited about my self discoveries and then life gives me another slap in the face. Then I yelled, "that's it!" I almost gave up because in my limited vision I couldn't see the forest for the trees. Then I remembered I had a choice. Well that helped to take some of the pressure off and dropped the decision right in my lap! No guilt, etc. I hadn't realized just how close I had come to leaving this planet. We have lots of invisible layers around us that we cannot see and the last layer for negative energy to work it's way into, is the physical body. If you have any physical ailments, pay attention to all you have just read.

It can be reversed. It takes a real desire and understanding to get there. At that time, I felt like it would be easier to escape my body. Then someone very dear to me said, "don't go." Well, as you can see I didn't.

I have a very curious nature and I like to turn over all the rocks to see what's underneath. Of course, I could get bit! Then, I saw the least flickering of hope. What if I missed out on something really beautiful? I mean just about the absolute greatest. I always taught my kids not to give up. You just don't know what might be around the next corner. Spark that curiosity. Don't be afraid of the pain. We can and will turn this world around. Some people are saying it's all going to end in 2012. Not for me! I intend to be here in 2025. My granddaughter, Annie, just looked at me in a very curious fashion when I told her that. We make our own destiny, with guidance from the Divine. Do you really think all this hard work is going to go down the drain? I plan on being around!

How about you? All you need is stability; which is the ability to come to center. (balance) It's just a new beginning. Don't buy into the concept of the chicken little story of, "The Sky is Falling." Chicken little is hit on the head with something hard and he thinks that the sky is falling. He goes around telling everyone, 'the sky is falling!" Everyone gets all excited and soon begins to live in fear. Soon he is told that it was something else that hit him on the head and the sky was still there! He forgot to look up! Now does that sound familiar? The earth is coming to an end, we're all going to die, and the sky is falling. That is just to give you a little analogy and some food for thought. The more we change our negative attitude into a positive attitude, the more we change the world and ourselves. You are free to choose one of the above!

The Laughing Buddha

The Laughing Buddha, see how he
smiles
How far he travels cannot be measured
in miles

His wisdom we know and his joy when
he see's
The games that we play, with laughter
and glee

How curious to find him, laughing you
see
Do I know him, does he know me

His love we know of, from where did he
come
The light in his eye's, it comes from the
sun

So when you do wonder what his secret
is
Just smile in your heart and there it is...

Living / Dying

Sometimes we feel like life's not worth it. We get that feeling because we are unable to trust. We should be living life to the fullest every day. I was watching a program on television and on the program it was remarked, "not living life to the fullest was like spitting in God's eye!" I tell you it keeps happening! Look and for the messages. Things are not put before us just by chance. We have to pay attention, listen closely and watch. We have to open our hearts and renew our trust. Why? Because it was either stolen from us, or we lost it ourselves, or maybe both. Maybe it's not necessary to know all the details now. We need to teach our children joy. If we are not living in joy, at least some of the time, how do we expect them to live that way? We can create miracles. I help at the senior center and when I see someone who is not smiling I make a special effort to smile at them. It may be their only joy that day. Stay gentle and it will be passed back to you. If you find yourself angry, (who me?) take a deep breath and blow it away. Do not let it reside in your energy field. In case you already forgot, it will make you sick. Take charge of your life and dump that garbage you are carrying. Put it in the nearest dumpster and not in you. Keep the rose pink cloud, no garbage allowed. Sing that to remind you! We are learning how to become "Gentle Warrior's." Now, you are really learning how to take your power back! Start teaching yourself, now that you have the power to control what goes on in your life. (or should I say, allow) The more you practice the more you change, here we go with that balance thing.

  Now when the really ugly things happen, how do you deal with them? You turn it over to your higher power. Ask them to please see you through this. Remember it's not your job to judge or forgive. It does help you to learn about forgiveness but true forgiveness will automatically come into being when you are able to stand in the light. Think of standing in the spotlight and the light space getting bigger and bigger around you as you envision God's love. Another method that works for me some of the time, is when I come to an abrasive situation or person, I just close my eye's and I send love darts to the Christ center or seed of creation in that person or persons. Do not look at the outer parts. It is not necessary for anyone to know. Their higher self will either accept it or reject it and you will not be interfering with their free will.

My sister Shirley is a retired teacher and was very experienced in handling problems. This particular time she couldn't resolve the problem with this one person and was having a lot of trouble getting along with her. She had tried everything. She knew about the book I was writing and the things I was learning. We had a conversation about the problem and I told her about sending the love darts. My sister has a lot of love in her and she did this. She called me back soon after and told me that it really worked. (no, the darts cannot have sharp points) See how we can really make a difference!

Most of us say we are not afraid to die and that comes from our inner faith. The crossing over to the other side can be very quick or sometimes it may take longer. Somewhere in the back of our minds, we know. I believe that we came into this world with a contract. We have certain things we agreed upon so we could evolve and grow spiritually. I also believe there are many other choices that are left up to us. For example, what we do with the situations we are faced with. If you continue to play the " Ping Pong" game, it will go on and on until you get it right. If you choose not to play the game, at least some of the time, you will have begun to realize the futility of it. Maybe I am over-simplifying it. I now know how to get out of most situations, if I can keep my mouth shut! Where we go after we quit playing the game here on earth is up to you to search out in your own heart. Notice I said heart, not head! I feel that when we have balanced ourselves in unconditional love, we will have arrived. Picture this; everyone living in unconditional love would be a little like 'heaven here on earth." Most comments I hear are, 'I wonder what heaven is like?" Again, I don't pretend to have all the answers. What we need to do is strengthen our happy moments. No, it isn't easy, but if you are sincere and ask for help, you will get it. The minute we have a negative thought we snap right back into our old habits. It comes down to a choice as to where you want to be. My positive moments are getting a little longer each day. I am recognizing the old patterns when they come up. I can now say to myself 'don't go there," out loud, or in my own mind and mean it! The next stage I have to really practice on is my thought patterns. Many times I have not listened and said," I will do it all by myself." Why do we continue to choose the hard way? It is beginning to be so pleasant to release and allow and let the Angels, who are under God, clear the way. They seem to be so much better at it than I am. Let's stop chasing our tails. Let's think! Let's be free and grow!

Friendship

Friend on mine, where are you

close by as to feel my need

when things are darkest, you are there

If only in my mind

a voice from within, sent from the

how silent, yet so clear

friendship, without words conveyed

through paths unknown

this God given gift, friendship

I return to thee

Remember, you choose! This side or that, positive or negative, light or darkness. Let's look and open our hearts for new answers and guidance. There is a plan and a purpose. It is revealed to us as we are ready to understand it. Learn that trust, is your best friend. We will brighten our light and help others. We only have to take one tiny step at a time. We are at a point in our evolution, where we are so weary and tired of fighting. We want to live in joy. Some have already arrived. Welcome to a new beginning!

Heart Hope / Soul Truth

When I think of hope from the heart, I
see a crystal clear vibrant white light.
When I get discouraged or depressed, I
think of the light connection and I renew
my hope. Thus we have, 'heart hope."
This is the reaching out to others from
the heart. I actually feel the sensation of
stretching, or as you will, giving or
sending pure love energy. Now that's a
lot of light! No shadow! This is what
keeps us going and helps us not to give
up. Start peeling those layers that have
been covering up your heart. Open that
beautiful flower. Let it breathe. Be
gentle with yourself and others.
Everyone is so fragile. We do not want
to hurt ourselves or anyone else. It's
against our true nature. * (One way that
really helps to keep me in line are my
tapes.) I find them to be invaluable to
my self discipline and spiritual growth. I
have learned so much from them and
can better discipline my mind, so that it
*(see acknowledgements)

is not always running off in all directions.

What is soul love? Soul love is the love from Spirit that is in all of us. This is what I believe remains, after we die and leave the physical body. These are terms that I can understand for now. It is a struggle. It's just a matter of wheth er you will answer the call of your soul. You will only do this if you want to. There is no mistaking the unbelievable pull. This is what I had been searching for and nothing was going to stop me! It's as simple as that! At least on paper. If you desire it, it will happen. Our soul draws us to the light. Are you tired of the word light? Substitute the words, divine spark, pure joy, peace and harmony or any other words you choose. When you pass this on it grows like the leaves and branches of a never ending, never ceasing, tree of life, (I was wondering where that was) bearing fruit for all who wish to partake! We have been asking for a long time for answers. How do we stop the pain and sorrow of this world? It is in our hands with divine guidance, and from those who have gone before us; God, Masters, Angels, guides, teachers and whoever else may be out there shining their light for us. It's time now to pick up all those beautiful thoughts and blessings that are awaiting our awakening. The paths are being opened, more now than ever before. Reach if you will. Ask if you will. We can help each other. We are the branches and the leaves. We have the power to change. We will make it happen in ourselves. Take 'Heart / Hope" with you everywhere. St art to cry less and let go of the pain. Allow the great ones to help us help ourselves.

May the peace that passes all understanding

be with you today and forever,

from this day forward

www.ingramcontent.com/pod-product-compliance
Lightning Source LLC
Chambersburg PA
CBHW020343290526
45785CB00005B/2150